BRITAIN'S CENTURY
SPORT

Press Association

BRITAIN'S CENTURY

SPORT

MAINSTREAM
PUBLISHING

EDINBURGH AND LONDON

First published in Great Britain in 1999 by
MAINSTREAM PUBLISHING COMPANY (EDINBURGH) LTD
7 Albany Street
Edinburgh EH1 3UG

ISBN 1 84018 286 5

A catalogue record for this book is available from the British Library

Typeset in Gill Sans Light
Printed and bound in Great Britain by Butler & Tanner Ltd

May Sutton Bundy, the first American to win the ladies' singles championship at Wimbledon, pictured in action in 1907. She was born in Plymouth, Devon, but moved with her parents to California, at the age of six. She won the title twice, continued playing tennis until she was 85 and died of cancer, aged 88, in 1975.

Lady archers in competition, 1908.

The start of the 100 kilometres cycle race at the Olympic Games in London, 1908.

Italian Dorando Pietri about to break the tape to win the 1908 London Olympics Marathon. Pietri was later disqualified for being assisted by his manager while in a state of collapse.

Competitors in the 1908 London Olympics Marathon leaving Windsor for London.

Charles B. Kingsbury of England after winning the
20 kilometres track cycle race at the London Olympic
Games in a time of 34 minutes, 13 seconds, July 1908.

The 1909 Oxford and Cambridge boat race.

Dr W.G. Grace (right), the famous cricketer, playing bowls, *c.* 1911.

The scene after the finish of the Derby in 1911, won by Sunstar.

The King's horse Anmer, ridden by H. Jones, in the parade prior to the 1913 Derby. During the race a suffragette, Emily Davison, threw herself under this horse and died several days later from her injuries.

The scene after the suffragette incident involving Emily Davison during the Derby in 1913: H. Jones, the jockey of the King's horse, is carried away with injuries.

Wimbledon, 1913: Mrs Lambert Chambers in play.

The Countess of Drogheda, during a ladies' golf match between the House of Lords and the House of Commons at Bishop's Stortford, 1913.

Tee hee! 'Prime Minister of Mirth', comedian George Robey, playing golf, c. 1913.

Crystal Palace: panorama of the 1914 FA Cup final between Burnley and Liverpool. Burnley won 1–0.

Cup final at Crystal Palace, 1914 between Burnley and Liverpool. Freeman (Burnley), near the penalty spot, scores the only goal of the match. This was the first cup final to be attended by a reigning monarch (George V).

The Pearly King of Hoxdon with a Pearly Prince and a Pearly Princess on the course at the Derby, 1914.

Derby Day, 1914.

On Christmas Day hostilities ceased in favour of football. Here, officers and men of the 26th Divisional Train, ASC, enjoy a game at Salonika during the First World War, December 1915.

Jimmy Wilde, flyweight boxing champion of the world, training, 1918.

Steve Donoghue winning at Epsom on Lady Phoebe, 1919.

French tennis ace Suzanne Lenglen, the ladies' singles champion, playing at Wimbledon, June 1920.

Boxer Tommy Noble in 1920, when he won Tex Rickard's featherweight belt. Noble was reputed to have earnt £100,000 from the ring. He died in London in 1966, aged 68.

The scene at Wembley Stadium for the 1923 FA Cup final, in which West Ham defeated Bolton Wanderers 2–0. King George V (foreground, right) is watching the action.

British athletes march past the royal stand during the opening ceremony of the Olympic Games in Paris, July 1924.

Eric Liddell winning the 400 metres flat race at the Olympic Games in Paris, 1924.

Major H.O.D. Segrave (left) with his mechanic after winning the 200 mile race at Brooklands, September 1925.

Jack Hobbs and Herbert Sutcliffe take the field at the Oval to open the batting for England in the final Test against Australia, August 1926.

Hobbs gets one away, despite the number of close fielders, during the third day of the Test at the Oval, August 1926.

Spectators cheer wildly as the players come out onto the pavilion balcony at the Oval in 1926 after England defeated Australia to win the Ashes.

The Prince of Wales, on Miss Muffit II, jumps a fence during the Household Brigade Steeplechase, 1928.

The start of the 1929 Grand National, showing the record number of starters at Aintree.

Some of the field taking Becher's Brook during the 1929 Grand National.

H.W. 'Bunny' Austin in action at the Wimbledon men's singles tennis tournament, 1929.

Don Bradman smacks I.A.R. Peebles to leg on the second day of the fifth Test match between England and Australia at the Oval, 1930. 'The Don' went on to make 232 in this innings, helping Australia to win the Test and the whole Ashes series.

Don Bradman and Stan McCabe going out to bat during the third Test match between England and Australia at Leeds, July 1930.

The Australian fielders form a circle around Jack Hobbs as he arrives to open England's second innings, on the fourth day of their Test match at the Oval, 1930 The cheering, led by Australia's Bill Woodfull, was a salute to Hobbs, who was about to bat for the last time in a Test match.

The Duke of Gloucester shaking hands with H. Hibbs of England, before the international soccer match between England and Scotland at Wembley, April 1930.

David Jack (left), captain of England, shakes hands with Scottish captain Davie Meiklejohn before the kick-off in the 1930 soccer international at Wembley. The referee is Williams McLean from Belfast. England won 5–2.

Footballers Alex James (left) and Cliff Bastin of Arsenal, 1930.

King George V attending the FA Cup final at Wembley, 1930. He shakes hands with the Arsenal team before the start of the match.

Alex James scores for Arsenal in the first half against Huddersfield Town in the 1930 FA Cup final. Wembley's famous towers loom in the background. Arsenal won the game 2–0.

Chelsea player Andy Wilson taking a cigarette before the match against Manchester City at Stamford Bridge, London, November 1930. Chelsea won the game 2–0.

Spain playing international soccer at Highbury, London, December 1931. Zamora, the Spanish goalkeeper, saves from Dixie Dean; but Spain were defeated by England.

Herbert Chapman, Arsenal
Football Club manager, 1932.

England defeat Scotland 3–0
at Wembley, April 1932:
E. Blenkinsop (left) and N. Dewar
vie in a duel for the ball.

Facing page top: NCU meeting at
Herne Hill, 1932, featuring the
one mile 'ordinary' scratch race.
The 'ordinary' bicycle is more
commonly known as the penny-
farthing.

Facing page bottom: Clive Dunfee,
who was killed during a race at
Brooklands in a 130 mph crash,
1932. Picture shows the car about
to start off in the race. The owner,
Mr Barnato, is seen second from
right.

Australia v. England, February 1933: England's Harold Larwood bowling to a tightly packed leg-side field during the infamous 'bodyline tour' of 1932–33. Australian batsman Richardson hits this one over the top, but Australia lost this Test in Brisbane and the series too.

The Everton footballers who defeated Manchester City at Wembley returning home to Liverpool, May 1933. Dixie Dean, the Everton captain, is in the carriage window at Euston with the FA Cup.

Sir Malcolm Campbell with his new Bluebird car, 1933.

As a result of a wager, Mr Samson, claiming to be the strongest man in the world, holds together a pair of shire horses at Croydon, June 1933.

E.C. Fernihough on an Excelsior JAP 175 cc motorcycle, at the Brooklands race track, 1933.

Gordon Richards on Elsenor, winning the Mitre Selling Plate at the Hurst Park racecourse, 1933, to equal Fred Archer's record of 246 winners.

A great little man dwarfed by his police escort: Gordon Richards at Hurst Park racecourse after riding his 246th winner.

Players of Chelsea FC at Euston Station, 1934. Hughie Gallacher is centre wearing bowler.

World table-tennis champion and British lawn tennis hero, Fred Perry, shown in action at Wimbledon, 1934. Some years later he moved to America and took US citizenship.

Members of Arsenal FC, 1935. Left to right: Bastin, Drake, Male, Hapgood and Copping.

Cliff Bastin (right) of Arsenal tries a flying shot against Bolton at Highbury, London, May 1937.

Cambridge University defeat
Oxford University in the wartime
boat race at Henley. This race,
during the Second World War,
was the first held at Henley since
the inaugral boat race in 1829.

Famous football internationalists (left to right) Stanley Matthews, Stanley Mortensen (both Blackpool) and George Hardwick (Middlesbrough), taking part in an instructional film made the by Football Association at Hendon, 1947.

Tommy Lawton (left), pictured in 1947. An English football legend, he established a reputation for being one of the most formidable centre-forwards in a prolific goalscoring career either side of the Second World War. He won 23 England caps, scoring 22 goals.

England's Denis Compton hits out at a bouncer from Australia's Ray Lindwall during the first day of play in the third Test match at Old Trafford, Manchester, July 1948. Compton was 64 not out at the end of play, despite suffering a facial injury. The match ended in a draw.

Top right: Footballer as well as cricketer, Denis Compton trains at Arsenal's Highbury Stadium, London, 1949.

Manchester United captain Johnny Carey is carried on the shoulders of his team-mates after they won the FA Cup final of 1948 against Blackpool.

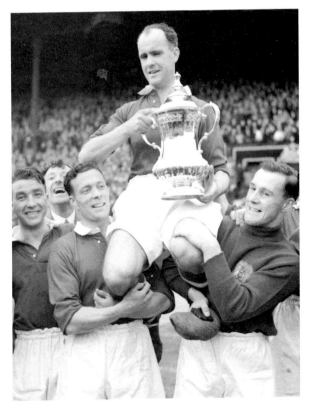

Competitors get off to a start in the marathon event at the Empire Stadium, Wembley, August 1948.

England and Kent wicket-keeper Godfrey Evans in action against the West Indies at Trent Bridge, May 1950. Evans played 91 Tests for England between 1948 and 1959 and was regarded as one of the all-time greats behind the stumps. But the West Indies had a strong touring side, winning this Test by 10 wickets and the series 3–1.

England captain Alf Ramsey leads his team onto the pitch at Roker Park, Sunderland, for their international against Wales, November 1950. England won 4–2. Sir Alf Ramsey, who later managed England to World Cup glory in 1966, died in 1999, aged 79.

Sugar Ray Robinson (left) throwing a long left to the head of eventual victor Randolph Turpin during their world middleweight title bout at Earls Court in London, July 1951. The two met again the following September in New York, when Robinson knocked out Turpin in the tenth round to regain his title.

Figure skater Jeanette Altwegg of Liverpool practises for the first time following a knee injury at the Streatham Ice Rink, London, October 1951. She went on to win a gold medal in the Winter Olympics at Oslo, 1952.

An early picture of jockey Lester Piggott, dated February 1952.

Daniel, the Welsh centre-half, hits the turf in front of Scottish centre-forward Reilly, during a Wales v. Scotland soccer international at Ninian Park, Cardiff, 1952. Scotland won 2–1.

The supreme moment for Blackpool outside-right Stanley Matthews (right) and his captain and centre-half Harry Johnston as both are chaired by jubilant team-mates after their 4–3 win over Bolton Wanderers in the 1953 FA Cup final at Wembley.

Champion jockey Gordon Richards celebrates his coronation knighthood with his first Derby winner, riding Sir Victor Sassoon's Pinza to victory at Epsom, 1953.

Red-headed Sam Bartram, veteran Charlton Athletic goalkeeper and captain for the day, runs out with the ball for his 500th, and record, league appearance with Charlton. Their match was against Portsmouth at the Valley Ground, South London, March 1954.

Oxford, May 1954: twenty-five-year-old medical student Roger Bannister hits the tape at an athletics meeting and the world's first sub-four-minute mile has been run. Despite a 15 mph crosswind gusting to 25 mph, Bannister completed the distance in 3 minutes, 59.4 seconds.

Stirling Moss in his Maserati after winning the Aintree 200 motor race, 1954.

Britain's Chris Chataway beats Soviet ex-sailor Vladimir Kuts to win the 5,000 metres at the London v. Moscow athletics event and set a new world record in the European games, at the White City Stadium, London, October 1954.

Thirty-four-year-old Bill Pickering of Bloxwich, Staffordshire, is greased down before entering the water at St Margaret's Bay, Dover, for his attempt to swim the Channel, August 1955.

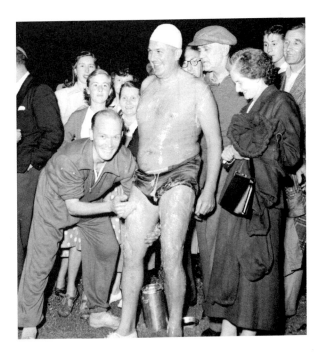

Golfer Henry Cotton during the second day of the Dunlop Masters golf tournament at Little Ashton, September 1955.

Watched by opponent John Pulman, Joe Davis breaks off at the start of the first match in a snooker tournament at Burroughes Hall, London, January 1956.

Leading Brighton and Hove Albion on to the field of play against Gillingham is 22-stone comedian Fred Emney, complete with monocle and cigar for his BBC TV series, *Emney Enterprises*.

Manchester City captain Roy Paul holds aloft the FA Cup supported by his team after they beat Birmingham City 3–1 in the final at Wembley, 1956.

Juan Fangio of Argentina takes a well-earned drink after winning the British Grand Prix in a Ferrari, at Silverstone, July 1956.

Manchester United manager Matt busby with his 'Babes' (left to right): Albert Scanlon, Colin Webster, John Doherty, Tony Hawesworth, Alec Dawson and Paddy Kennedy. United's team plane crashed at Munich airport on the return flight from Belgrade in February 1958.

Tom Finney, England and Preston North End forward, in a shower of water which almost completely hides Chelsea left-back Bellet as they tussle for the ball on the soaked pitch at Stamford Bridge, London, August 1956.

Duncan Edwards of Manchester United, pictured in April 1957.

Bill Marsten is up for the Cup in 1957, blowing his own trumpet on behalf of Manchester United in London's Trafalgar Square.

Wreckage of the BEA Elizabethan airliner which crashed in Munich on February 1958 when bringing home members of Manchester United's football team from a European Cup match in Belgrade. Only 12 survived out of 40 aboard.

Billy Liddell, Scottish internationalist and pin-up boy for Liverpool fans during the 1950s. Over a thousand supporters demonstrated at Anfield in 1959 when Liverpool temporarily dropped him from the first team. Dunfermline-born Billy had been signed from Lochgelly Violet in 1939.

Bob Roden from West Gorton, Manchester, jumps for joy at the prospect of seeing his beloved Manchester United at Wembley Stadium against Bolton Wanderers in the 1958 FA Cup final. But United were beaten 2–0.

Chelsea FC full-back Terry Venables, 17 years old, with band leader Joe Loss rehearsing at the Hammersmith Palais, London, for his début as a singer, December 1960.

Tottenham Hotspur captain Danny Blanchflower holds the FA Cup as he is carried by his team-mates after their 2–0 victory over Leicester City in the 1966 final at Wembley. Tottenham also achieved the 'double', as League champions.

Wimbledon, 1961: beaten but smiling, Christine Truman puts a friendly arm around Angela Mortimer, first British winner of the ladies' singles title since 1937.

Stirling Moss, driving a Lotus, takes Woodcote Corner on the Goodwood circuit during a test, May 1963.

Airborne Chelsea goalkeeper Peter Bonetti turns the ball round the post to concede a Liverpool corner during the FA Cup semi-final at Villa Park, Birmingham, March 1965. But 'the Cat' was beaten twice as Liverpool eventually won 2–0.

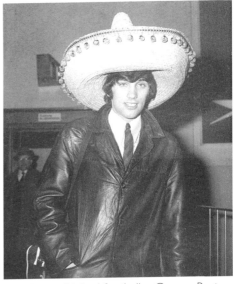

Manchester United footballer George Best wearing a souvenir sombrero on his return to London following United's defeat of Benfica 5–1 in the second leg of the European Cup quarter-finals, March 1966. Best scored United's first two goals.

Boxer Cassius Clay (Muhammad Ali), accompanied by Jimmy Ellis (left), during an early-morning training session, jogging to his workout in Hyde Park before the heavyweight clash against British champion Henry Cooper, May 1963.

Right: Blood pours from the face of Henry Cooper as the referee stops the world championship fight in the sixth round at Arsenal's Highbury Stadium, London. Cassius Clay (Muhammad Ali) retained his title.

The Chair jump resembles a battlefield during the 1966 Grand National at Aintree, Liverpool, as Jockey J. Speid-Coote hangs grimly to the reins of his mount Black Spot, and jockeys P. Cowley (left) and J. Magee (centre, by fence) lie on the brush-strewn turf.

The new British Open champion, Jack Nicklaus, of Columbus, Ohio, kisses the trophy after winning his title at Muirfield, East Lothian, 1966.

England's Geoff Hurst cracks a shot past German goalkeeper Hans Tilkowski to score the last goal in the World Cup final against West Germany at Wembley, 1966.

England's triumphant 1966 World Cup final captain Bobby Moore chaired by hat-trick hero Geoff Hirst (left) and Ray Wilson as he brandishes the Jules Rimet Trophy after their 4–2 victory over West Germany.

England international footballer Bobby Charlton reads a newspaper at the Royal Garden Hotel in Kensington, London, the day after he helped England win the 1966 World Cup at Wembley Stadium.

Foinavon, ridden by John Buckingham, lands confidently after sailing over the last fence in the 1967 Grand National, which he went on to win at 100–1.

Manchester United players (left to right) Alex Stepney, Pat Crerand and John Aston celebrate winning the European Cup at Wembley Stadium, London, by beating Benfica of Portugal 4–1 in the final, May 1968. Of course, United were not the first British team to lift this trophy. That honour went to Celtic's famous Lisbon Lions the previous year.

Jackie Stewart in the paddock at Silverstone in practice before the 1969 British Grand Prix.

Graham Hill at a luncheon given in his honour at the Savoy Hotel in London, the day after he had received the OBE at an investiture ceremony in Buckingham Palace, 1968.

Britain's triumphant Ann Jones in lawn tennis action, beating Australian Margaret Court in their ladies' singles semi-final on the centre court at Wimbledon, 1969. Glory followed in the final, with the defeat of title-holder Billie Jean King.

Lilian Board, Britain's 400 metre
silver medallist at the Mexico
Olympic Games, in action on the
athletics track, 1970.

Henry Cooper during his heavyweight championship fight of Great Britain with Joe Bugner, at the Empire Pool in St Ives, March 1971.

Wembley, 1971: Charlie George (left), who scored the winning goal, holds the FA Cup in celebration with Arsenal captain Frank McLintock following their defeat of Liverpool, 2–1 after extra time. With this win Arsenal completed the League and Cup double.

Arsenal fans standing in Upper Street, Islington, London, taste their team's victory as Frank McLintock holds out the FA Cup for them to touch. Arsenal had just won the 1971 final at Wembley.

Finding it rather warm, Princess Anne tips her top hat after competing in the dressage at the European Horse Trials in Burleigh, 1971.

Alan Mullery, the captain of Tottenham Hotspur, chaired with the UEFA Cup after their drawn match against Wolverhampton Wanderers gave them a 3–2 win on aggregate at White Hart Lane, London, 1972.

Lee Trevino of USA with the trophy after winning the British Open golf championship at Muirfield, 1972.

TV football pundit Jimmy Hill – also a qualified referee – running the line during the Arsenal v. Liverpool match at Highbury, London, September 1972. He stepped in, from the commentary box, when one of the official linesman had to retire with an injury.

Bill Shankly shows his delight to the Liverpool fans at Anfield after Liverpool drew with Leicester City 0–0 to win the 1972–73 First Division championship.

Scotland's captain Billy Bremner missing the best chance his team had for a goal during the drawn game against Brazil in the 1974 World Cup tournament in Frankfurt, Germany.

BRITAIN'S CENTURY

Facing page top: Legendary Welsh scrum-half Gareth Edwards gets the ball away from the scrum in a rugby union international at Cardiff Arms Park, March 1975: Wales beat Ireland in this match 32–4.

Facing page bottom: L'Escargot, ridden by Tommy Carberry, comes home to win the Grand National at Aintree, 1975.

Streaker hurdles stumps at Lord's during the England v. Australia Test match, August 1975. It was a hot summer.

Heathrow Airport, May 1976: Kevin Keegan, Gerry Francis and Mick Channon, members of the England football squad, head for Scotland and Hampden Park for the deciding game in the home international championships. Scotland won 2–1.

Joe Bugner raises his arms in victory after flooring Richard Dunn in the first round at the Empire Pool, Wembley, October 1976.

The crowd goes wild with joy as Red Rum, ridden by Tommy Stack, romps home at Aintree in 1977 to make National Hunt history as winner of the Grand National for a record third time.

Holding aloft the Challenge Trophy, which she received from the Queen, Britain's 31-year-old Virginia Wade acknowledges the applause on Centre Court at Wimbledon after beating Betty Stove of Holland in the ladies' singles final – British success in the Queen's Silver Jubilee year, 1977.

Britain's James Hunt after winning the 1977 John Player British Grand Prix in his Marlborough McLaren at Silverstone. Austria's Nikki Lauda was second, with Gunnar Milsson of Sweden third.

Yorkshire and England opener Geoff Boycott, having knocked up his 100th first-class century at Headingley during the fourth Test against Australia in August 1977, is engulfed by celebrating crowds. He lost his cap in the commotion, but a fan returned it before the resumption of play and Boycott went on to make 110 not out.

Barbarians full-back J.P.R. Williams tackled by British Lions right-wing Peter Squires in the Silver Jubilee rugby match at Twickenham, September 1977. The Lions won 23–14.

Liverpool captain Emlyn Hughes holds aloft the European Cup at Wembley Stadium, May 1978, after the Merseysiders beat Belgian champions FC Club Bruges 1–0. A Kenny Dalglish goal ensured Liverpool became the first British club to retain the trophy.

Scotland manager Ally MacLeod leaving the plane at Gatwick Airport after the unsuccessful team's return from the World Cup tournament in Argentina, June 1978.

Trevor Francis balances the European Cup on his head in the Olympic Stadium, Munich, after he scored the only goal to give Nottingham Forest victory over Malmo in the 1979 European Cup final.

Above: British athlete Sebastian Coe in action during the Golden Mile race at Bislett Stadium, Oslo, 1979. He won the race and in the process set a new world record for one English mile (3 minutes, 48.95 seconds).

Bristol's Robin Cousins, pictured in 1979 showing the skill that made him one of the world's best ice-skaters. He won a gold medal for figure skating at the 1980 Winter Olympics, Lake Placid, USA.

Swedish tennis star Bjorn Borg drops to his knees while acknowledging the applause of fans on Wimbledon's Centre Court after beating Roscoe Tanner to become the men's singles champion for a historic fourth successive year, 1979.

David Wilkie, pictured in 1980, four years after shattering the world record as he won Olympic gold in the 200 metres breaststroke at Montreal.

England rugby captain Bill Beaumont during the 1981 Calcutta Cup match against Scotland, at Twickenham. England won 23–17.

The start of the London Marathon in Greenwich Park, March 1981.

Garth Crooks and Ricardo Villa holding the FA Cup at a reception in Tottenham Town Hall, north London, after Spurs' FA Cup final victory over Manchester City at Wembley, 1981.

All-rounder Ian Botham celebrates a Test match wicket against Australia at the Oval in London, August 1981. His dramatic return to form during this Test series helped England secure the Ashes.

British athlete Daley Thompson in 1981, competing in the pole vault – one of the ten disciplines in the decathlon event for which he achieved Olympics success.

Kevin Keegan, pictured in 1981 with First Division football club Southampton, having returned to English football the previous year after a stint with Hamburg in West Germany. He joined Hamburg after a hugely successful spell with Liverpool.

Facing page top: The snowbound stakes at Newmarket, December 1981. Horses from a nearby stable are out exercising on a snow-covered heath after 14 days without racing in Britain due to the wintry conditions.

Facing page bottom: Two female fans streak on to the pitch topless during the 1982 rugby international match between England and Australia at Twickenham. Two policemen help to cover one of the exposed women, Erica Roe (left), and 69-year-old Ken Bailey of Bournemouth, known as 'World Cup Willie', holds his Union Jack over the other woman's exposed top.

Olympic and European ice dance champions Jayne Torvill and Christopher Dean in action during an ice-skating competition in London, April 1982.

Liverpool defender Alan Hansen in action in 1984. Alloa-born Hansen made 86 league appearances for his first professional club, Partick Thistle, before transferring to Liverpool.

Team captains David Gower and Clive Lloyd pictured, after the West Indies completed a clean sweep in the 1984 Test series, at the Oval. This was England's first five-Test whitewash in a home series.

A pall of smoke hangs over the main stand at the Valley Parade football ground as it is engulfed during the Bradford City v. Lincoln City match in May 1985. Over 50 people were killed and more than 200 injured.

Scotland's legendary soccer manager Jock Stein being carried from the touch-line by police after he collapsed and died as the final whistle blew on his team's World Cup tie with Wales at Ninian Park, Cardiff, September 1985. Scotland went on to the World Cup finals in Mexico the following year.

Victorious captain Tony Jacklin holds aloft the Ryder Cup presented to the European team after they defeated the USA at the Belfry, 1985.

Zola Budd acknowledges the crowd which applauded her breaking the women's 3,000 metre world record at Cosford, February 1986.

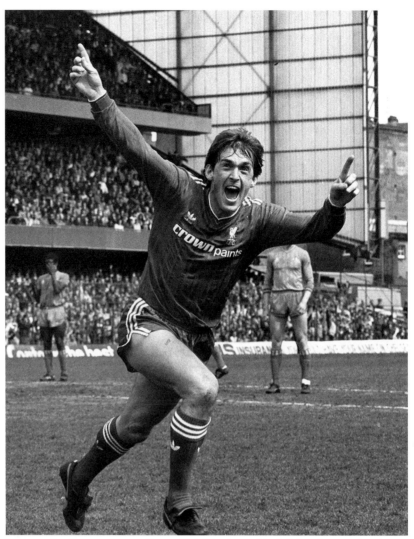

Liverpool's player-manager Kenny Dalglish shows his delight after scoring the winning goal in the 23rd minute of his side's vital Division One match against Chelsea at Stamford Bridge. The 1–0 victory clinched the 1985–86 First Division championship for Liverpool.

Ex-England international football team manager Glenn Hoddle in action for Tottenham Hotspur, November 1986.

Eye of the Hurricane: Alex Higgins applies concentration in the 1987 Benson and Hedges Masters snooker tournament at Wembley.

Flight of the Eagle: Eddie Edwards poses in London before jetting out to train with the American team prior to the 1988 Winter Olympics in Calgary.

Wimbledon manager Bobby Gould is crowned with the FA Cup and joined by his team at Wembley Stadium. From left to right: Eric Young, goal-scoring match hero Laurie Sanchez, goalkeeper Dave Beasant and Terry Phelan. Wimbledon beat Liverpool 1–0 in the 1988 final.

England winger Richard Robinson (centre) drives through the line-out as Australian captain Nick Farr-Jones sweeps the ball away during the opening Test match between England and Australia at Twickenham, November 1988.

Right: Desert Orchid is guided over the last fence by jockey Simon Sherwood and on to victory in the Tote Gold Cup Steeplechase at rain-soaked Cheltenham, 1989.

Thousands of fans, friends and families gather at Anfield Stadium around a pitch full of flowers for the ceremony of remembrance for all those who perished in the tragic Hillsborough disaster. Ninety-five were crushed to death because of overcrowding in the FA Cup semi-final between Liverpool and Nottingham Forest on 15 April 1989 at Hillsborough, Sheffield. A ninety-sixth fan died four years later in hospital.

Sheffield's Herol Graham (left) and New York's Mike McCallum feel each other's punching power during the vacant WBA world middleweight championship fight at the Royal Albert Hall, London, 1989. McCallum beat Graham on a split points decision.

Admiring glances from England cricketers Ian Botham (left) and Robin Smith as an unsupported Australian supporter invades the pitch at Old Trafford during the fourth Cornhill Test, England v. Australia, July 1989.

Scotland's Ally McCoist takes a shot at goal during the World Cup qualifier against Norway at Hampden Park, Glasgow in November 1989, which ended as a 1–1 draw.

Sally Gunnell of Great Britain celebrates after winning the women's 400 metres Olympic hurdles final in the Olympic Stadium, Barcelona, 1992.

Gary Lineker of Tottenham Hotspur looking positive after scoring against Coventry City at Highfield Road, Coventry, January 1991.

Former Nottingham Forest manager Brian Clough giving a thumbs-up after his team beat Tottenham Hotspur at the City Ground, Nottingham, December 1992.

Flamboyant boxer Chris Eubank showing a penchant for *haute couture* in January 1993. The top hat pictured was nearly 200 years old.

Former boxer Michael Watson at Highbury Stadium, London, to publicise his benefit football match in March 1993. His story reached national consciousness after he fell into a coma following a middleweight title fight with Nigel Benn.

Above right: Following the second false start of the 1993 Grand National, one of the course stewards waves a red flag to stop the race at Aintree. Later, the race was declared void and was not re-run that year.

Stephen Hendry poses with his trophy after winning the 1994 World Snooker Championship at the Crucible Theatre, Sheffield.

Damon Hill celebrates on the rostrum after driving his Williams Renault to victory in the 1984 British Grand Prix.

Ian Wright celebrates after scoring for Arsenal during their FA Premiership football match against Crystal Palace at Highbury. It was Wright's 100th goal for the club.

A piper leads Scotland's Colin McCrae and co-driver Derek Ringer with their Subaru Impreza on to the winners' rostrum after their victory in the 1994 RAC Rally which finished in Chester.

A dejected Scot, Scott Hastings, looks on as Will Carling celebrates at Twickenham, March 1995. England beat Scotland 24–12 to win the Grand Slam.

Sacked England skipper Will Carling makes an appearance, complete with mobile phone and bottle of champagne, outside his house in London, the day after he was sensationally stripped of the England rugby captaincy in May 1995.

Right: Delight for Jonathan Edwards as he breaks the world triple jump record in the 1995 World Championships in Gothenburg.

England captain Mike Atherton takes the long walk back to the pavilion after losing his wicket to the West Indies during the sixth Test match at the Oval, August 1995.

Above right: Nigel Benn swings a right at the head of challenger Danny Ray Perez during the WBC super-middleweight bout at Wembley Stadium, September 1995. Benn went on to retain his title.

Britain's Frank Bruno talks to the media at his training camp in Las Vegas during preparations for his forthcoming World Boxing Council title fight with American Mike Tyson, March 1996.

Facing page top: Matthew Pinsent (left) shakes hands with fellow Briton Steve Redgrave after winning a gold medal in the coxless pairs at the 1996 Olympic Games, Atlanta.

Facing page left: Paul Gascoigne celebrates his goal with Teddy Sheringham in the Euro '96 clash against Scotland, at Wembley. England won 2–0.

Facing page right: Linford Christie sprinting in round two of the 200 metres at the 1996 Olympics, Atlanta. Christie, who was disqualified from the 100 metres final, failed to qualify for the semi-finals, coming in fourth.

Jumping for joy, 1996: Frankie Dettori leaps from the saddle on Shantou after winning the final classic of the season, the St Leger, at Doncaster.

Launching her bid for heptathlon glory in the Athens 1997 World Championships, Denise Lewis of Great Britain wins the long jump to go into second place overall in the competition.

The triumphant 1997 European Ryder Cup team with their prestigious golfing trophy, after retaining it against the USA in Valderrama.

Racehorse strings still make their way through Middleham and its snow-covered rooftops on their way to Middleham Moor, despite the prolonged wintry conditions which made National Hunt racing impossible in northern England in early 1998.

Below left: Over and out as amateur jockey Joe Tizzard falls from Cherrynut at the final fence in the John Hughes Memorial Chase over the Grand National fences on the opening day of the Aintree meeting, April 1998.

Prince Naseem Hamed holds up his belt after beating Puerto Rica's Wilfredo Vazquez to retain his WBO featherweight title at Manchester's Nynex Arena, April 1998.

Arsenal boss Arsène Wenger poses with the FA Cup and Premiership trophy as the team take a victory tour from the Highbury ground to Islington Town Hall, to celebrate winning the 1997–98 double.

English forward Michael Owen (right) celebrates with team-mate David Beckham after scoring the equaliser at Toulouse during the 1998 World Cup Group G match between England and Romania. But Romania won 2–1, their winning goal coming in the 90th minute.

Tim Henman celebrates a point in his match against Patrick Rafter which he won 6–3, 7–6, 3–6, 6–2, to go into the quarter-finals at Wimbledon, 1998.

David Beckham is given the red card during England's World Cup match against Argentina at St Etienne, 1998. Argentina won this clash 4–3 on penalties, after extra time, to go into the quarter-finals.

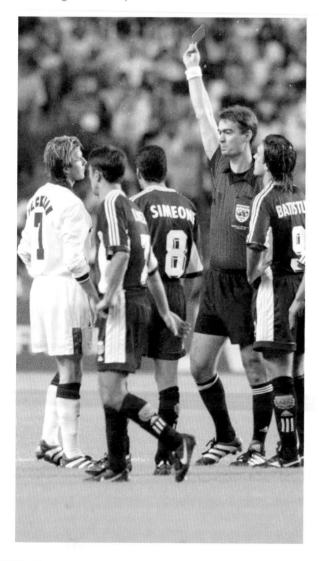

Facing page top: Britain's Colin Jackson goes over the hurdle during his 110 metres hurdles heat at the 1988 European Championships in Budapest's Nepstadium. He qualified with 13.31 seconds.

Facing page bottom: A streaker enjoys a run around Silverstone during the 1998 British Formula One Grand Prix.

Huge crowds at Deansgate, Manchester, cheer the treble-winning Manchester United football team back from Barcelona in May 1999, as they ride an open-top bus with the three trophies.